Daughter...

*I want to give this to you,
to thank you for being
such a joy to my heart.*

Also by Douglas Pagels

Chasing Away the Clouds

*Everyone Should Have a Book like This
to Get Through the Gray Days*

*Everyone Should Have a Book like This
to Remind Her How Wonderful She Is*

*For You, Just Because
You're Very Special to Me*

I Want You to Read This Today...

A Keepsake for My Children

100 Things to Always Remember...

Required Reading for All Teenagers

30 Beautiful Things That Are True About You

To the One Person I Consider to Be My Soul Mate

All writings are by Douglas Pagels except as noted.

Library of Congress Control Number: 2005905273
ISBN: 978-1-59842-112-5

Certain trademarks are used under license.
BLUE MOUNTAIN PRESS is registered in U.S. Patent and Trademark Office.
Acknowledgments appear on page 4.

Printed in the United States of America.
Second Printing: 2007

 This book is printed on recycled paper.

This book is printed on fine quality, laid embossed, 80 lb. paper. This paper has been specially produced to be acid free (neutral pH) and contains no groundwood or unbleached pulp. It conforms with the requirements of the American National Standards Institute, Inc., so as to ensure that this book will last and be enjoyed by future generations.

Blue Mountain Arts, Inc.
P.O. Box 4549, Boulder, Colorado 80306

Every
DAUGHTER
should have
a book
like this
to remind her
how wonderful
she is

Douglas Pagels

Blue Mountain Press
Boulder, Colorado

ACKNOWLEDGMENTS

We wish to thank Susan Polis Schutz for permission to reprint the following poem in this publication: "You can depend on..." from TO MY DAUGHTER, WITH LOVE, ON THE IMPORTANT THINGS IN LIFE. Copyright © 1986 by Stephen Schutz and Susan Polis Schutz. All rights reserved.

We gratefully acknowledge the permission granted by the following authors, publishers, and authors' representatives to reprint poems or excerpts from their publications.

Hyperion for "A dozen of our friends were in..." by Winston Groom from BIG SHOES by Al Roker. Copyright © 2005 by Al Roker. All rights reserved. And for "There is a part of me that wants to..." and "Know that I am your greatest ally..." from LETTERS TO OUR DAUGHTERS by Kristine Van Raden and Molly Davis. Copyright © 1999 by Kristine Van Raden and Molly Davis. All rights reserved. Reprinted by permission of Hyperion.

G.P. Putnam's Sons, a division of Penguin Group (USA), Inc., for "Daughters never really leave their mothers..." from A LOTUS GROWS IN THE MUD by Goldie Hawn. Copyright © 2005 by Illume, LLC. All rights reserved.

Scribner, an imprint of Simon & Schuster Adult Publishing Group, for "She is anything anyone could ever..." from DON'T MAKE ME STOP THIS CAR! by Al Roker. Copyright © 2000 by Al Roker. All rights reserved.

Carol Lynn Pearson, www.carollynnpearson.com, for "Mother, if I did not grow up to be..." from WILL YOU STILL BE MY DAUGHTER, published by Gibbs Smith. Copyright © 2000 by Carol Lynn Pearson. All rights reserved.

Simon & Schuster Adult Publishing Group for "I pray every day that I can be..." from LETTERS TO MY DAUGHTERS by Mary Matalin. Copyright © 2004 by Mary Matalin. All rights reserved.

HarperCollins Publishers for "If you become a bird and fly away..." from THE RUNAWAY BUNNY by Margaret Wise Brown. Copyright © 1942 by HarperCollins Publishers. Text copyright renewed 1970 by Roberta Brown Rauch. All rights reserved.

Harry N. Abrams, Inc., New York, for "I bless the day she came..." by Judy Swank from HOLLYWOOD MOMS by Joyce Ostin. Copyright © 2001 by Joyce Ostin. All rights reserved.

A careful effort has been made to trace the ownership of selections used in this anthology in order to obtain permission to reprint copyrighted material and give proper credit to the copyright owners. If any error or omission has occurred, it is completely inadvertent, and we would like to make corrections in future editions provided that written notification is made to the publisher:

BLUE MOUNTAIN ARTS, INC., P.O. Box 4549, Boulder, Colorado 80306.

Contents

Remember How
the Proverb Goes...

Parents hold their
children's hands
for a while...
and their hearts
forever.

— Old Proverb

I wish I could find the words
to tell you how great it is to be
the parent of a daughter like you.

The perfect words would tell you
how proud I am of all you've done
and everything you've become.

The ideal words would say
what a joy it was to watch you
grow up, and what an amazing
and rewarding and loving
experience it continues to be.

Every time I see you, I know that
I am looking at as beautiful a gift
as anyone has ever been given.

And I know that I could have hoped and
prayed and dreamed all my life... and
I could have wished on a million stars.

But I couldn't have been blessed with
    anyone more wonderful...
        than the daughter
            that you are.

Daughter,
Thanks for All the Smiles
You've Given Me

I want you to know how much you're
treasured and celebrated and quietly thanked.

I want you to feel really good...
    about who you are.
About all the great things you do!
I want you to appreciate your uniqueness.
Acknowledge your talents and abilities.
Realize what a beautiful soul you have.
Understand the wonder within.

You make so much sun shine
through, and you inspire so much
joy in the lives of everyone who is
lucky enough to know you.

You are a very special person,
giving so many people a reason to
smile. You deserve to receive the
best in return, and one of my
heart's favorite hopes is that the
happiness you give away will come
back to warm you
    each and every day of your life.

I have so many lasting memories, favorite thoughts, and special smiles that were all made possible... by you. There are very few people on earth who understand how much these treasures mean to me, but you are a daughter who understands so much of what family and love and togetherness are all about.

And I want to thank you for
        making it all so rewarding.

Through all the best moments of life, from holding you in my arms when you were little to holding you in my heart every moment, I have always felt like I was the luckiest parent in the world... and someone whose sweetest dreams did more than become a reality.

One of the nicest things that could happen to anyone... happened to me. I've been able to not only raise a beautiful daughter, but also to watch a miracle in the making.

And that lovely miracle
        ...is you.

Remember What Winston Said...

A dozen of our friends were in the waiting room outside, and I heard the cheer go up all the way down the hall as soon as somebody announced, "It's a girl!"

...The years since have passed so quickly, life seems to have become like one of those time-lapse pictures of a growing flower.

— Winston Groom

A Little Note with
a Lot of Love

You are such a precious, extraordinary person.
It's just amazing to see the things you're
growing up to be. You impress me so much
with all the things you've learned, all the
things you care about, and all the things
you understand.

You know that it's all about making the most
of your life and of the time you have been
given. About doing the best you can do —
and letting go of the things that are beyond
your control.

It's about believing in tomorrow and
stretching your wings. Embracing your
blessings and appreciating all the sweet
memories you have made...

It's about reaching for your stars, brightening your days, and filling your heart in a thousand ways.

It's about lifting up others, sharing the road, and continuing down the path on the way to making things better than they were before. It's about taking the next step into whatever lies ahead. It's about finding out that you'll never need to feel alone, and that your family, your faith, your hopes, and your dreams will be with you forever.

And it's about remembering, no matter what, that you'll always be the most welcomed and wonderful part of... a special place called home.

Remember What
Susan Said...

You can depend on
my support, guidance
friendship and love
every minute of every day

— Susan Polis Schutz

Sometimes we need reminders in our lives of how much people care. If you ever get that feeling, I want you to remember this...

I love you, Daughter.

Beyond words that can even begin to tell you how much, I hold you and your happiness within my heart each day. I am so proud of you, and so thankful to the years that have given me so much to be thankful for.

If I were given a chance to be anything I wanted to become, there's nothing I would rather be... than your parent.

And there is no one
I would rather have
...as my daughter.

What a Beautiful Blessing You Are

One of the nicest things anyone can ever be
blessed with... is the splendid gift of
a daughter like you.

You are the angel of my life.

I wish I could tell you that every day. Maybe this
little book can help me say that for now. And I'm
hoping it will remind you of those words and that
exquisite feeling every time you see it in the years
to come.

In every single one of the seasons of your life, you
have been the sweetest thing in mine. You were the
most beautiful baby girl any parent ever held in
their arms. You were the most treasured toddler,
the prettiest little girl, and the source of a million
smiles all the way through every year in school.
And you just continue to impress and amaze me
in so many ways. I know you always will.

We have shared so much together, you and I.
I have spent more moments than you will ever
know... hoping, praying, worrying, wondering,
reminiscing about the past, projecting into the
future, and always — always — feeling incredibly
privileged that the gift of being the parent of
someone as magnificent as you... was a present
that was given to someone as thankful as me.

You are on my mind so often. I think about our
joys, our tears, our talks, our hugs. Our bond that
has been with us from the very beginning and that
continues on — so strong and loving — to this
very day. All those things... are my favorite things.
They're my life's most beautiful memories and
treasures and prizes.

You have always been my angel.

And thinking of you now, and remembering you
back then, it's pretty wonderful to realize
    that halos seem to come... in all sizes.

You are so deserving of every good thing that can come your way. And I want you to know, if I could have a wish come true, I'd wish for every day of your life to be blessed with some special gift that warms your heart, some gentle smile that touches your soul,
and so many things that simply take your breath away.

Remember What
This Says...

Life is not
measured by
the number of
breaths we take,
but by the
moments that
take our
breath away.

— Anonymous

May You Remember...

Daughter, in your happiest and most exciting moments,
   my heart will celebrate and
      smile beside you.
In your lowest lows, my love will be there
   to keep you warm, to give you strength,
   and to remind you that your sunshine
      is sure to come again.
In your moments of accomplishment,
   I will be filled so full of pride
   that I may have a hard time keeping
      the feeling inside of me.
In your moments of disappointment,
   I will be a shoulder to cry on,
   a hand to hold, and a love that
   will gently enfold you until
      everything is okay.
In your gray days, I will help you search,
   one by one, for the colors of the rainbow.

In your bright and shining hours, I will
    be smiling, too, right along beside you.
In your life, I wish I could give you a very
    special gift. It would be this:
    When you look in the mirror in the years
    ahead, may you smile a hundred times
    more than frowning at what you see.
    Smile because you know that a loving,
    capable, sensible, strong, precious person
        is reflected there, each and every day.

And when you look at me, may you
    remember how very much I love you...
    and how much I'll always care.

Remember What Goldie Said...

Daughters never really leave their mothers, and thank God for that. I couldn't imagine my life without her to share it with.

— Goldie Hawn

I want you to know that I would
gladly drop whatever I'm doing,
at any time of the day, just to have
a chance to give you a hug, and
to say how much I care,
and to share a few precious
moments with you.

Right this very minute, I'd love
nothing more than to be with
you, looking at the smiling
face of someone who has inspired
so many smiles in my life.

I think of you all the time.

And even when we're not together,
I take comfort in knowing that
the caring and closeness between us
    will never change,
        and that you'll always be
            in my heart.

A Little Prayer
I'd Love to Share
with You

I want your life to be
    such a wonderful one.
I wish you peace. Deep within
    your soul.
Joyfulness. In the promise of
    each new day.
Stars. To reach for. Dreams.
    To come true.
Memories. More beautiful
    than words can say...

I wish you friends. Close at heart,
    even over the miles.
Loved ones. The best treasures
    we're blessed with.
Present moments. To live in,
    one day at a time.
Serenity. With its wisdom.
    Courage. With its strength.
New beginnings. To give life a
    chance to really shine.

I wish you understanding. Of how
    special you really are.
A journey. Safe from the storms
    and warmed by the sun.
A path. To wonderful things.
An invitation. To the abundance
    life brings.
And an angel watching over.
        For all the days to come.

Something for My
Beautiful Daughter
to Remember Forever

Has anyone told you lately what an exquisite person you are?

I hope so! I hope you've been told dozens of times... because you are just amazing.
And just in case you haven't heard those words in awhile, I want you to hear them now. You deserve to know that...

It takes someone special to do what you do. It takes someone rare and remarkable to make the lives of everyone around them nicer, brighter, and more beautiful. It takes someone who has a big heart and a caring soul. It takes someone who's living proof of how precious a person can be.

It takes someone... just like you.

Remember What
Al Said...

She is anything anyone
could ever want
in a daughter.

— Al Roker

As the Years Go By

I remember how I used to tuck you in at night.
One of the sweetest jobs in the universe is giving
a kiss and a hug and saying how much "I love you"
to a sleepy child who thinks that "one more story"
might be just about right. I remember weekends
and pushing you in the swing and watching you
reach for the sun and the moon and every star
in the sky.

As time passed so quickly, and as you grew, I
remember how you couldn't wait to show me
the project or the picture of the day as soon as
I'd see you after school. Even though your
backpack was almost as big as you were, you
never had any problem carrying all your things...
and all my dreams for you... on those strong
shoulders of yours.

I remember all the times I worried about you
being gone too long from my sight. I remember
the sweet feeling of seeing you again, even if it
had only been a few hours since we'd been apart...

I remember thinking at least a million times what a joy you are to me, and wondering how anyone could love someone as much as I love you.

The precious feeling remains with me right up to this very day. I am simply amazed at how the seasons have flown by, and at how you have grown up so quickly... right before my eyes. When I look at you, I see someone I cherish. I see someone I love with every smile, every hope, every prayer, and every treasured memory within me. When I look at you, I see someone who has so many paths yet to walk, opportunities to explore, and stars to keep on reaching for.

As the years go by, my hopes will travel beside you on all your journeys. My heart will still wish you sweet dreams at night, and you will be a joy to me... all of your life.

Remember What Kristine Said...

There is a part of me that wants to stop the clock right now. I want to keep you safe and protect you. I want to tuck you in night after night.

But I know that I cannot protect you, just like my mother knew, and hers, and hers. What I must continue to do instead is to teach you, guide you, honor you, and respect you...

I'll love you eternally.

— Kristine Van Raden

Every family has its own special universe that it revolves in. But each one, too, is subject to certain universal truths. One of them is about children and their ability to push the fast-forward button on the passage of time.

Many of my friends and neighbors weighed in on the subject, but the "elders" in my family were probably the first ones who notified me of the fact that children "grow up so fast." I guess it was a concept that was confirmed by watching the likes of me, and it led to a bit of generational wisdom they passed along when you were born. I bet it had been told, with a smile and a sigh, by their parents to them, in much the same fashion.

But Kristine's got it right. There comes a time when one has to stop worrying about the time flying by and concentrate more on today and how to make tomorrow the best it can be. And when you have a daughter who's a walking miracle on the way to a wonderful life, you want to do everything you can — while you can — to honor her by getting it right.

20 Beautiful Things
That Are True
About You

You are something — and someone — very special.
You really are. No one else in this entire world is
exactly like you, and there are so many beautiful
things about you.

You're a one-of-a-kind treasure, uniquely here in
this space and time. You are here to shine in your
own wonderful way, sharing your smile in the best
way you can, and remembering all the while that
a little light somewhere makes a brighter light
everywhere. You can — and you do — make a
valuable contribution to this world.

You have qualities within you that many people
would love to have, and those who really and truly
know you... are so glad that they do. You have a
big heart and a good and sensitive soul. You are
gifted with thoughts and ways of seeing things that
only special people know. You know that life doesn't
always play by the rules, but that in the long run,
everything will work out.

You understand that you and your actions are capable of turning anything around — and that joys once lost can always be found. There is a resolve and an inner reserve of strength in you that few ever get to see. You have so many treasures within — those you're only beginning to discover, and all the ones you're already aware of.

Never forget what a treasure you are. That special person in the mirror may not always get to hear all the compliments you so sweetly deserve, but
   you are so worthy of
      such an abundance
         ...of friendship, joy, and love.

If Anyone Knows,
It's Me

It is wondrous when a child comes into your life and inspires every single thing to become more beautiful, more meaningful, more precious, and more of all the things dreams are made of.

Until you came along, I never would have imagined the joy I'd come to know. Until I was given the privilege of watching you grow into the unique, one-of-a-kind wonder that you are, I never could have imagined the depth of pride I'd feel inside.

If anyone has learned how much love a heart can hold, it's me. I'm so thankful that you're my daughter, and I'm so lucky that you're in my life.

Remember What
Carol Said...

"Mother, if I did not grow to be just like you, are you disappointed?"

The mother looked up...

"Oh, no," she said. "You are *you*, and you are better than I ever dreamed."

— Carol Lynn Pearson

To My Amazing, Remarkable Daughter

Everywhere you journey in life, you will go with my love by your side.

Forever it will be with you. Truly, joyfully, and more meant to be than words could ever say. You are the joy of my life, the source of my dearest memories, the inspiration for my fondest wishes, and you are the sweetest present life could ever give to anyone.

I love you so much. I want you to remember that... every single day. And I want you to know that these are things I'll always hope and pray...

That the world will treat you fairly. That people will appreciate the one-in-a-million person you are. That you will be safe and smart and sure to make good choices on your journey through life...

That a wealth of opportunities will come your way. That your blessings will be many, your troubles will be few, and that life will be very generous in giving you all the happiness and success you deserve.

You're not just a fantastic daughter. You're a tremendous, rare, and extraordinary person. All the different facets of your life — the ones you reveal to the rest of the world, and the ones known only to those you're close to — are so impressive. And as people look even deeper, I know they can't help but see how intrinsically beautiful you are.

I'll always love you with all of my heart. And I couldn't be more proud of you... if I tried.

Remember What Mary Said...

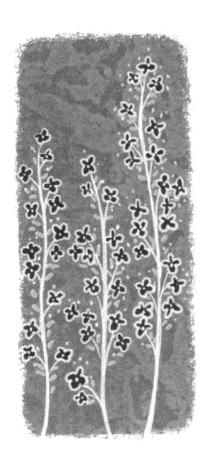

I pray every day that I can be your best mom for all time. Someone you can lean on for today's stubbed toe and tomorrow's bruised ego. Someone who can make sure that that laugh-out-loud glee that came with your first extraordinary, training-wheel-free, two-wheeler experience is there for all your life experiences to come.

— Mary Matalin

These Are the Gifts
I'll Always Wish for You

Happiness. Deep down within.
Serenity. With each sunrise.
Success. In each facet of your life.
Close and caring friends.
Love. That never ends.

Special memories. Of all the yesterdays.
A bright today. With much to
    be thankful for.
A path. That leads to beautiful tomorrows.

Dreams. That do their best to come true.
And appreciation. Of all the wonderful
        things about you.

Always and Forever

Daughter, may you always be patient with the problems of life, and know that any clouds will eventually give way to the sunlight of your most hoped-for days. May you be rewarded with the type of friendships that get better and better — and the kind of love that blesses your life forever.

May you find happiness in every direction your paths take you. May you never lose that sense of wonder you have always had, and may you hold on to the sense of humor you use to brighten the lives of everyone who knows you. May you go beyond the ordinary steps and discover extraordinary results. May you keep on trying to reach for your stars, and may you never forget how wonderful you are...

May you meet every challenge you are faced with, recognize every precious opportunity, and be blessed with the knowledge that you have the ability to make every day special. May you have enough material wealth to meet your needs, while never forgetting that the real treasures of life are the loved ones and friends who are invaluable to the end. May you search for serenity, and discover it was within you all along.

May you be strong enough to keep your hopes and dreams alive. May you always be gentle enough to understand. May you know that you hold tomorrow within your hands, and that the way there will be shared with the makings of what will be your most precious memories.

When It's Time to Fly

There are so many new horizons ahead. In the blink of an eye, daughters are off to college, off to jobs, and eventually on to setting up their own homes and tending to their families and future lives. It's a time when parents hope and pray that all the values and lessons they tried to instill will help to light the way for the journey ahead.

And I am no exception: I want great things for you, too... and I have an enormous amount of faith in your ability to make your life a happy one. You take with you, everywhere you go, a supply of confidence, common sense, ability, determination, understanding, wisdom, and so many attributes that just sparkle inside you. You know how to make the right choices, and I know that you will.

But of all the things you take with you, you should know that you also leave something behind. Some people call it an "empty nest," but in its own special way, there's nothing empty about it. It will always be abundantly filled with wishes, support, hugs and hopes, an open line of communication, a close and caring bond, a sense of belonging, and a strong and constant love.

Remember What
Margaret Said...

If you become a bird
and fly away from me...
I will be a tree
that you come home to.

— Margaret Wise Brown

Once Upon a Time

These days, the things that people read are sometimes in books, but just as likely to be in magazines and on computer screens. But once upon a time, you and I spent so many perfect moments curled up together reading words just like those of Margaret Wise Brown's. We filled our home with those timeless books, and those stories warmed our hearts. When you were little, it was a very big thing to me to have that special kind of togetherness blessing our lives.

As the years have passed, I find that it's not just birds that fly... time does, too. And now the things I read aren't about runaway bunnies or saying good night to the moon. And I haven't seen a favorite bear there, pretending to be a rain cloud, when I go to turn the page. There used to be genies, hungry caterpillars, and wild things whisking our imaginations away, but these days our world is filled with so many different things.

The stories of our lives in the present day have pages, too. If we could read them now, they'd probably sound pretty sedate to some people, but they've been a grand adventure to me. I hope you'll feel the same way, every day, about your life.

As the pages fill up, I hope your life story takes you every special place you've ever dreamed of. Just remember, Daughter, no matter where you go any time you "fly away," there will always be a place that you can come home to.

No matter how long any journey turns out to be, I know that you will never forget which path to take... to come home to me. I will always be here with open arms, incredibly thankful for our closeness and our caring. And whether we're chatting while we're stirring up something in the kitchen, taking a long walk with a lot of catching-up to do, or just relaxing on the porch on some summer's day that's still years away, I'll always look forward to having you share each one of *your* stories... with me.

Remember What
Charles Said...

I celebrate... the day
that gave me such a dear
and good daughter as you.

— Charles Dickens

It would bring me more joy than I can say
if you would never forget
    — not even for a single day —
how wonderful you are...
    in my eyes and in my heart.

I'm so often at a loss to find the words to
tell you how much you mean to me. In my
imagination, I compare you with things like
the sunshine in my mornings, the most
beautiful flowers in the fields, and the
happiness I feel on the best days of all.

You're like the answer to a special prayer.
    And I think God knew
        that the world needed
            someone exactly like you.

A Few Words
from the Heart

There is never a day that goes by without my thinking of what a beautiful blessing you are to my life. God must have been smiling down on me... when you came into the world. And I promise you this: it would be a far less fantastic, rewarding, and remarkable place... without you.

I am so enormously proud of you! I love you beyond all words that I will ever be able to say, and I will love you every moment.

There are gifts that are far above
    priceless.
There are memories that are made
    of pure love.
There are special miracles that
    really do come true.

And all my life, you
    will always be...
a wonderful gift, a treasure of
    memories, and an amazing
        miracle... to me.

If there is ever a time when I can help in any way, with anything, I want you to know, my daughter, that you can turn to me.

It doesn't matter what it is… when it is… or where the two of us may be. What does matter to me is your well-being, your highest hopes, and your sweetest dreams.

I want that big, beautiful heart of yours to be filled with as much happiness as it can hold. I want the world to be so good to you! I want it to give you an abundance of love and warmth and wonder… because that's exactly what you deserve to receive.

So please remember this:
You can always count on me to be here for you, cheering you up, cheering you on, and just being there to love you and to listen and to gently understand.

Remember What
Molly Said...

Know that I am your greatest
ally and fan. I will continue
to applaud at your victories
and walk with you through
trials and mistakes...

I'll love you forever.

— Molly Davis

In this crazy world we live in, it's nice to know that some things will never change…

No matter what is happening in the world.
No matter what worries or frustrations creep in.
No matter what glad or sad tidings come your way.
No matter how many bills come in the mail.
No matter how good or bad the news of the day.
No matter whether the weather is beautiful or not.
No matter how many times your smile gets lost.
No matter how difficult or demanding things can be.
No matter what is happening anywhere at any time…

You will always be in my heart. You will always be in my thoughts. And I'll always be wishing I could find a way to remind you... that you are the most marvelous daughter there could ever be.

I know that life can be hard sometimes, and that the world can be a crazy place. But I want you to remember that the two of us will always do what we can to make things better... and my love will walk beside you, from now until forever.

Remember What Judy Said...

I bless the day she came to me...
Through the years
she made me laugh so hard
I cried.
She shared her dreams.
She shared her heart.
We shared the risks.
We share our love.
And she taught me courage
to find my way.
What beautiful, joyful
moments we have had —
    me and my little girl...

— Judy Swank

I'd like to share this thought
with you, to tell you that
    you mean the world to me.

Think of something you couldn't
    live without
    ...and multiply it by a hundred.
Think of what happiness means to you
    ...and add it to the feeling you get
        on the best days you've ever had.

Add up all your best feelings
and take away all the rest...
    and what you're left with is
        exactly how I feel about you.

You matter more to me than you can
    imagine and much more than I'll ever
        be able to explain.

May You Always Have an Angel by Your Side

May you always have an angel by your side ✝ Watching out for you in all the things you do ✝ Reminding you to keep believing in brighter days ✝ Finding ways for your wishes and dreams to take you to beautiful places ✝ Giving you hope that is as certain as the sun ✝ Giving you the strength of serenity as your guide ✝ May you always have love and comfort and courage ✝ And may you always have an angel by your side ✝

May you always have an angel by your side ✝ Someone there to catch you if you fall ✝ Encouraging your dreams ✝ Inspiring your happiness ✝ Holding your hand and helping you through it all ✝

In all our days, our lives are always changing ✶ Tears come along as well as smiles ✶ Along the roads you travel, may the miles be a thousand times more lovely than lonely ✶ May they give you gifts that never, ever end: someone wonderful to love and a dear friend in whom you can confide ✶ May you have rainbows after every storm ✶ May you have hopes to keep you warm ✶

✶ And may you always have an angel
by your side ✶

Remember... I'll always love you. Remember... as you hold this in your hands and read these words, that I'll hold you in a very precious place in my heart — as long as there are stars in the sky.

Remember that — if I could — I would give you the moon and the sun in return for all the smiles and memories you've given me.

And remember that when I say "I love you," I want you to know what those words really mean. "I love you" means that you're the most wonderful daughter there could ever be. It means that you have made me more proud of you than you could even begin to imagine. And it means that I will never let a day go by without feeling blessed by the giving... of a gift like you.

Remember What
James Said...

Dearest daughter…
to you I send
the biggest kiss
that ever was.

— James Russell Lowell

Daughter, do you know what my favorite things in the whole world are?

They all seem to start with having you as such a precious part of my life.

It's listening to a voice that has changed from first words and the littlest sighs to words that now share the deepest feelings and the strongest trust. It's the memories made — shaped through the days and captured on every sunlit path we were given the grace... of walking together.

It's the birthdays, the holidays, the special days. It's knowing that you are reason enough to celebrate every day. It's cherishing the way our lives entwine. It's the listening that always leads to more closeness...

It's learning that nothing could ever be more valuable than our companionship and the constant bond that endears us to each other. It's me, watching from the sidelines, quietly bursting with pride, seeing the process of a beautiful flower unfolding before my eyes.

Daughter, the smiles you give me are such magnificent gifts. And I just can't help but think: Someone else can win the lottery... and get all the prizes waiting to be won. Others can take their exotic travels, buy their mansions, and spend their entire lives adding to their worth.

I'm perfectly content to just close my eyes and to lovingly realize that, thanks to you...

I feel like the luckiest person
on earth.

And Remember
What I Said...

I am so blessed by the
thousands of smiles we
have shared, by the
memories we have
made, and by the way
you will always be such
a precious part of
everything that home
and love and family...
will *ever* mean to me.

— Douglas Pagels

You've always known that you are my world.

And I hope this book has been able to tell you some of the reasons why. A few of the thoughts are things you are hearing for the first time. Others are things I've tried to say (in my own special way) and share with you all your life. And there are other thoughts that you and I will share in days ahead, when all the right words and the perfect moments come along.

Until then, let me close by just saying...

Thank you. What an honor it has been. Watching such a beautiful person blossom. Someone I admire and adore with all my heart. Thank you for enriching my life beyond belief. Thank you for the grace and the goodness, the hopes, the memories, and the happiness. Thank you for bringing so many priceless gifts to me.

I love you so much.

About the Author

Bestselling author and editor Douglas Pagels has inspired millions of readers with his insights and anthologies. People of all ages and all walks of life are drawn to his work because they share so much with him: the same caring and concern, the same hopes and dreams, and so many of the same feelings. His writings have been translated into seven languages due to their global appeal and inspiring outlook on life, and his work has been quoted by many worthy causes and charitable organizations.

He and his wife live in Colorado, and they are the parents of college-age children. Over the years, Doug has spent much of his time as a classroom volunteer, a youth basketball coach, an advocate for local environmental issues, a frequent traveler, and a craftsman, building a cabin in the Rocky Mountains.